IN MY WEAKNESS GOD IS STRONG:

DECLARATIONS OF STRENGTH

SUSAN J PERRY

SIXTY-DAY DEVOTIONAL

*"GOD said it,
I didn't!
He told me to tell you!"*
~ Susan J Perry ~

Nehemiah 8:10
Then he said unto them, Go your way,
eat the fat, and drink the sweet, and
send portions unto them for whom
nothing is prepared: for this day is
holy unto our LORD: neither be ye
sorry; for the joy of the LORD is your
strength.

INDEX

DEVOTION

Our devotion and dedication is unto the Lord God Almighty as many are weak today and some die. We come to declare with them that when they are weak God is strong in every way. He never sleeps or slumbers and He loves and cares for us in totality. So today as we go forward let's declare our devotion to the Almighty God of Israel who was and is and is to come. He will be our strength. He is our Healer and Deliverer and there is no other.

Our strength must come from the Word of God and all that He is; we must love and trust Him today. When we define devotion, we find our hearts are in Christ. Where do we go without the Lord? The Bible says we live and have our being in Him:

Acts 17:28
For in him we live, and move,
and have our being; as certain also of your
own poets have said, For we are also his
offspring.

We intend for this 60-day devotional to help you find your strength again and falter no more as God is your strength and our devotion in Him; of Him, through Him in every way will change your life. Now come to the River of

Joy and find your strength as it returns to you each and every day.

The KJV Bible has 307 scriptures on strength for our lives to be edified and uplifted. Let's declare some of them each day to go forth stronger and stronger in the Word of God. Devote some time in the Word and know God's strength is for you. We are going to start out in Psalms and Proverbs, two of the wisdom books of the Bible and glean your joy and strength for each day. We will use various others from many books of the Bible to complete our sixty-day endeavor as well. God bless you as you declare strength unto yourself in every way.

De·vo·tion

/dəˈvōSH(ə)n/

noun

1. Love, loyalty, or enthusiasm for a person, activity, or cause: "His courage and devotion to duty never wavered."

DAY ONE

Psalm 8:2
*Out of the mouth of babes and sucklings hast thou ordained **strength** because of thine enemies, that thou mightest still the enemy and the avenger.*

God has made us strong even against our enemies today. He has ordained your strength against them. So let's declare this today:

"I declare I am strong and God gives me strength against my enemies!"

IN JESUS NAME!

GOD'S BEST
IS
YOU BLESSED!

DAY TWO

Psalm 18:1
*I will love thee, O LORD, my **strength.***

Loving the Lord will bring joy and strength to you for He is everything you need each day. So let's declare this today:

"I declare that I love the LORD and there is no other that gives me strength!"

IN JESUS NAME!

GOD BUILDS
HE DOESN'T
TEAR DOWN!

DAY THREE

Psalm 18:2
The LORD is my rock, and my fortress, and
*my deliverer; my God, my **strength**, in*
whom I will trust; my buckler, and the horn
of my salvation, and my high tower.

God gives us everything we need to be strong
as we go forth in Him as each scripture shows
us the way. So let's declare this today:

"I declare the Lord is my rock, my
fortress as He delivers me and gives me
strength, I can trust Him and He will
save me!"

IN JESUS NAME!

GOD IS LIGHT
AND
THERE IS NO DARKNESS
IN HIM!

DAY FOUR

Psalm 19:14
Let the words of my mouth, and the
meditation of my heart, be acceptable in thy
*sight, O L*ORD*, my* **strength***, and my*
redeemer.

God will give us strength through our words to
carry on as I meditate on what is acceptable to
Him. So let's declare this today:

"I declare that my words coming out of
my heart are acceptable unto the Lord
because He gives me strength as my
redeemer!"

IN JESUS NAME!

GOD FORGIVES
ALL
SIN!

DAY FIVE

Psalm 20:2
Send thee help from the sanctuary,
*and **strengthen** thee out of Zion;*

God will help us at all times no matter where
we are or what we are doing, He is our
strength. So let's declare this today:

**"I declare that the Lord will send me
help in the sanctuary and strengthen
me through His church!"**

IN JESUS NAME!

GOD IS STRONG
WHEN
YOU ARE WEAK!

DAY SIX

Psalm 20:6
*Now know I that the LORD saveth his anointed; he will hear him from his holy heaven with the saving **strength** of his right hand.*

The Lord will save His people those anointed for service unto Him. We will hear Him from Heaven as His strength will save us by the power of His right hand. So let's declare this today:

"I declare the Lord will anoint me and strengthen me today with His saving strength by His right hand!"

IN JESUS NAME!

GOD HAS OVERCOME
THE WORLD
MADE US OVERCOMERS TOO!

DAY SEVEN

Psalm 21:1
*The king shall joy in thy **strength**, O LORD;*
and in thy salvation how greatly shall he
rejoice!

Even the king shall rejoice when given joy and
strength in the Lord. Our President should
also in this day and age. Even high officials
need strength to govern the people and he will
rejoice and so shall you. So let's declare this
today:

"I declare I will rejoice as my king
rejoices as our strength and joy are
found in the Lord and He gives us our
salvation!"

IN JESUS NAME!

GOD IS FULL
OF
JOY &
THERE IS NO SADNESS
IN HIM!

DAY EIGHT

Proverbs 18:10
*The name of the LORD is a **strong***
tower: the righteous runneth into it, and is
safe.

The Lord is strong enough for all of us and His
name is too. We speak the name of Jesus and
we know in that name we will find strength
throughout our day. So let's declare this today:

**"I declare I am strong as I declare the
Lord's name is a strong tower, I can
run into it and be safe!"**

IN JESUS NAME!

GOD IS
MIGHTY
IN BATTLE!

DAY NINE

Isaiah 40:29
He giveth power to the faint; and to them
*that have no might he increaseth **strength**.*

In Isaiah he brings another point of view from
the eyes of the Prophet who wrote many
verses on strength also. We can glean in His
field as well. So let's declare this today:

**"I declare if I do not faint as my might
weakens, the Lord will increase my
strength!"**

IN JESUS NAME!

GOD SHALL COME TO US
LIKE
THE RAIN!

DAY TEN

Isaiah 40:31
*But they that wait upon the L*ORD *shall renew their* **strength***; they shall mount up with wings as eagles; they shall run, and not be weary; and they shall walk, and not faint.*

There are many ways to wait upon the Lord and He will take good care of you. This scripture personifies that deed in so many different ways. I marvel at this scripture, how about you? So let's declare this today:

"I declare if I wait upon the Lord, He will renew my strength and then I will fly like the eagle not get tired and I shall run and walk and never get faint!"

IN JESUS NAME!

GOD'S SON
IS
JESUS!

DAY ELEVEN

Psalm 22:19
But be not thou far from me, O LORD: O
*my **strength**, haste thee to help me.*

How much strength does the Lord have to give
out? He won't neglect you in any way, just cry
out to Him, Lord give me strength! So let's
declare this today:

"I declare hurry O Lord to give me
strength and be not far from me so you
may help me!"

IN JESUS NAME!

LOOK IN THE MIRROR
YOU ARE CREATED
IN
GOD'S IMAGE!

DAY TWELVE

Psalm 27:1
The LORD is my light and my salvation;
whom shall I fear? the LORD is
*the **strength** of my life; of whom shall I be*
afraid?

Father will never forsake you but give you the light of your salvation and He will strengthen your life and there is no one for you to fear as God is the center of your life. So let's declare this today:

"I declare the Lord is the light of my salvation and I will not be afraid and He will strengthen my life with His!"

IN JESUS NAME!

GOD'S PRESENCE
IS
ALL AROUND YOU!

DAY THIRTEEN

Psalm 27:14
Wait on the LORD: be of good courage, and he
*shall **strength**en thine heart: wait, I say, on*
the LORD.

Father always gives us a plan and a purpose
for our lives and here He tells you to wait. We
must be obedient to reap Father's benefits and
have patience. So let's declare this today:

"I declare that I must wait on the Lord
by being courageous and He will
strengthen my heart in the waiting!"

IN JESUS NAME!

LIVE THE GOD-KIND OF LIFE!

DAY FOURTEEN

Proverbs 10:29
The way of the LORD is **strength** *to the upright: but destruction shall be to the workers of iniquity.*

The Lord will strengthen you in every difficulty life presents to you and you will walk strong before Him again and again. So let's declare this today:

"I declare the Lord will strengthen me today as I walk upright in His ways!"

IN JESUS NAME!

YOU WILL REAP
WHAT
YOU SOW!

DAY FIFTEEN

Psalm 29:11
*The LORD will give **strength** unto his people;*
the LORD will bless his people with peace.

The Lord will strengthen us day by day
because we are His people who believe on
Him and love Him. There is nothing too great
the Lord will not do for us and we must be
thankful. So let's declare this today:

**"I declare the Lord will strengthen His
people and bless them with peace!"**

IN JESUS NAME!

SOW
ONLY GOOD
THINGS!

DAY SIXTEEN

Psalm 16:11
Thou wilt shew me the path of life: in thy
presence is fulness of joy; at thy right hand
there are pleasures for evermore

God is continuing to show us the way if we
stay close to Him and open to His movements.
In our obedience we will find the strength day
to day to grow in His ways. So let's declare
this today:

"I declare the Lord will show me the
way in life and in His presence I will
find the fullness of joy and at His right
hand, pleasures for eternity!"

IN JESUS NAME!

GO THE
EXTRA MILE
GOD WILL
BE WAITING!

DAY SEVENTEEN

Psalm 37:39
But the salvation of the righteous is of
*the LORD: he is their **strength** in the time of*
trouble.

The Lord helps us whenever we are in need
even if it is daily. Therefore this devotion
should help all of us as we proclaim our
strength in the Lord. So let's declare this
today:

***"I declare that my salvation comes
from the Lord and only He is my
strength in the time of trouble!"***

IN JESUS NAME!

DON'T GET
WEARY
GOD NEVER
SLEEPS
NOR SLUMBERS!

DAY EIGHTEEN

Psalm 41:3
*The LORD will **strength**en him upon the bed of languishing: thou wilt make all his bed in his sickness.*

The Lord God is our Healer, our strength and our buckler and when we believe that we can receive the strength only He can give supernaturally, we become strong. So let's declare this today:

"I declare Lord, you will strengthen me even when I am sick in my bed and wasting away I will live!"

IN JESUS NAME!

TRUST GOD
AND BE
SAFE!

DAY NINETEEN

Psalm 43:2
*For thou art the God of my **strength**: why*
dost thou cast me off? why go I mourning
because of the oppression of the enemy?

During stressful times we can look to the Lord
for our strength especially in the battle against
our enemies who try to defeat us and oppress
us, Jesus is the way. So let's declare this today:

"I declare that during my darkest
times fighting the enemy of oppression,
Lord you will not cast me away but
give the strength I need to endure this
battle!"

IN JESUS NAME!

GRIEF DOES
NOT LAST
JOY
COMES IN
THE MORNING!

DAY TWENTY

Psalm 46:1
*God is our refuge and **strength**, a very*
present help in trouble.

God is at our side during every trial of our life
and is ready to help you and I if we but ask.
Have you asked Him for help lately? So let's
declare this today:

**"I declare God is my refuge and my
strength in all times and especially
when I need help because I am in
trouble!"**

IN JESUS NAME!

COME TO
JESUS
TODAY!

DAY TWENTY-ONE

Psalm 59:17
*Unto thee, O my **strength**, will I sing: for*
God is my defence, and the God of my mercy.

The Lord will strengthen you through your
praise and worship unto Him in every
circumstance. One scripture says lift up holy
hands and praise the Lord. So let's declare this
today:

**"I declare as I sing my praises unto the
Lord who will defend me and give me
mercy; He will strengthen me through
this!"**

IN JESUS NAME!

GOD SEARCHES
THE
HEART!

DAY TWENTY-TWO

Psalm 68:28
Thy God hath commanded
*thy **strength**: **strength**en, O God, that*
which thou hast wrought for us.

God is sovereign and He will care for His people and He will build you up in strength so you can enjoy life. So let's declare this today:

"I declare God has built strength just for me and commanded it to come!"

IN JESUS NAME!

KNOW
JESUS
AND
YOU WILL
KNOW THE
FATHER!

DAY TWENTY-THREE

Psalm 23:1
The LORD is my shepherd; I shall not want.

I believe the Lord is our shepherd and if we follow Him, He will direct us as His flock of believers and take good care of us. This verse says we will not want. So let's declare this today:

"I declare the Lord is my shepherd and I shall not want for anything as He cares for me, He will strengthen me!"

IN JESUS NAME!

ASK FOR
WISDOM
GOD GIVES
LIBERALLY!

DAY TWENTY-FOUR

Psalm 23:2
He maketh me to lie down in green pastures:
he leadeth me beside the still waters.

How many of you know that God is at work in your life at all times and He cares for you lovingly? So let's declare this today:

"I declare the Lord gives me strength by taking me to green pastures and leads me beside still waters giving me peace!"

IN JESUS NAME!

FAITH
COMES
BY
HEARING!

DAY TWENTY-FIVE

Psalm 23:3
He restoreth my soul: he leadeth me in the
paths of righteousness for his name's sake.

Psalm 23 is one of the most beautiful of all
time. David was so touched by God through
his shepherding his flock of sheep that this
reaches us today giving us the strength and
hope that we need. So let's declare this today:

"I declare the Lord will restore my soul
as He leads me on His paths of
righteousness for His name's sake, I
will find strength!"

IN JESUS NAME!

BE DOERS
OF THE WORD
NOT JUST
HEARERS!

DAY TWENTY-SIX

Psalm 23:4
Yea, though I walk through the valley of the
shadow of death, I will fear no evil: for thou
art with me; thy rod and thy staff they
comfort me.

The Lord as our Shepherd is so good to lead
and direct us into safety as this verse 4 speaks
of Psalm 23. So let's declare this today:

"I declare the Lord who is my Shepherd
will lead me through the valley of the
shadow and death will not come upon
me and will keep me from fearing evil.
His rod and staff comforts me as He
cares for me!"

IN JESUS NAME!

ANGELS
ARE CAMPED
AROUND YOU!

DAY TWENTY-SEVEN

Psalm 23:5
Thou preparest a table before me in the
presence of mine enemies: thou anointest my
head with oil; my cup runneth over.

I love this scripture as it is very pictorial to
me. I want you to picture this yourself as we
declare it together, because God is so good to
us! So let's declare this today:

"I declare my God will prepare a table
for me and my enemies shall be seated
there too. And the Lord will anoint my
head with oil and my cup will run over
again and again until we have
overflow!"

IN JESUS NAME!

SURELY, GOODNESS
AND MERCY
SHALL FOLLOW YOU!

DAY TWENTY-EIGHT

Psalm 23:6
Surely goodness and mercy shall follow me
all the days of my life: and I will dwell in the
house of the LORD for ever.

Many things follow us throughout our days,
but God gives us named angels to follow us
and protect us as He strengthens us in the
House of the Lord. Selah! So let us declare
this today:

"I declare there are angels following
me each day I live, named: Surely,
Goodness and Mercy and they will help
me and strengthen me to dwell in the
House of the Lord forever and ever!"

IN JESUS NAME!

THE LORD
WILL LEAD
YOU!

DAY TWENTY-NINE

Psalm 54:1
Save me, O God, by thy name, and judge me
*by thy **strength**.*

God will save you however He must and He will judge you as well but He will give you strength on a regular basis because you are known by His name. So let's declare this today:

"I declare that by God's name I will be saved and I will be judged by His strength all my days!"

IN JESUS NAME!

JESUS
IS THE
ONLY WAY!

DAY THIRTY

Psalm 62:7
In God is my salvation and my glory: the
*rock of my **strength**, and my refuge, is in*
God.

We can depend on the Lord to be strong
because He is our Rock, this is one of His
names and attributes. We know that God
never fails and He will protect us in every
way possible as He strengthens us. So let's
declare this today:

"I declare that the Lord is my rock and
my glory and in Him I find strength
and refuge always!"

IN JESUS NAME!

THERE IS GRACE
WAITING FOR YOU
AT GOD'S THRONE!

DAY THIRTY-ONE

Psalm 31:1
In thee, O LORD, do I put my trust; let me
never be ashamed: deliver me in thy
righteousness.

We know that we should trust the Lord in
everything and in our tests and trials we find
strength to go through and never be ashamed.
Because God will deliver us from every pit.
So let's declare this today:

**"I declare my trust is in the Lord who
never allows shame to come on me
because He delivers me from it because
of His righteousness!"**

IN JESUS NAME!

DON'T LET
THE ROCKS
CRY OUT
PRAISE GOD!

DAY THIRTY-TWO

Psalm 65:6
*Which by his **strength** setteth fast the*
mountains; being girded with power:

I believe we are strengthened by everything
God says and does in the past; in the present
and in the future as we trust in Him, we will
see others strengthened too. So let's declare
this today:

"I declare as the Lord sets the
mountains with His strength and binds
them with His power, so He can do this
for me also!"

IN JESUS NAME!

PUT ON
THE WHOLE ARMOR
OF GOD!

DAY THIRTY-THREE

Psalm 37:24
Though he fall, he shall not be utterly
cast down: for the LORD upholdeth him with
his hand.

God will pick us up when we fall because He is our Lord and Master. We shall never be totally down and out because the Lord retrieves His people and then He restores them as well. So let's declare this today:

"I declare the Lord will pick me up when I fall, forgive me and uphold me with His hand!"

IN JESUS NAME!

BLOW THE TRUMPET IN ZION: SOUND THE ALARM!

DAY THIRTY-FOUR

Psalm 71:7
I am as a wonder unto many; but thou art
*my **strong** refuge.*

God has made us His wonder to many as we
stay strong and do not bow down to others as
weapons are formed against us but will not
prosper. So let's declare this today:

"I declare I am God's wonder to the
world as He makes me strong because
He is my refuge!"

IN JESUS NAME!

THE LORD
WILL
PROVIDE!

DAY THIRTY-FIVE

Proverbs 14:26
*In the fear of the LORD is **strong** confidence:*
and his children shall have a place of refuge.

Many times in scripture it says God is our strong refuge and we have this place of safety within Him. Stay close and be safe. So let's declare this today:

"I declare in the fear of the Lord we have our confidence in Him as children of God gives us a place of refuge from all enemies!"

IN JESUS NAME!

GOD HAS
ALL
THE ANSWERS!

DAY THIRTY-SIX

Proverbs 24:5
*A wise man is **strong**; yea, a man of*
knowledge increaseth strength.

The Bible says in the Book of James that God
will give us wisdom liberally if we but ask.
Have you asked lately? We need wisdom for
every situation in our lives. So let's declare
this today:

"I declare God will strengthen me with
wisdom and knowledge as only He can
do from on High!"

IN JESUS NAME!

LOVE
ONE ANOTHER!

DAY THIRTY-SEVEN

Psalm 73:26
My flesh and my heart faileth: but God is
*the **strength** of my heart, and my portion*
for ever.

I know that God tends to our strength issues
in every facet of our lives after all He is the
creator isn't He? Our hearts must be kept
strong before the Lord because there is where
He searches you. So let's declare this today:

"I declare my flesh and heart may fail
but God will strengthen my heart
because He is my portion forever!"

IN JESUS NAME!

KEEP YOUR FOCUS ON JESUS!

DAY THIRTY-EIGHT

Psalm 78:4
We will not hide them from their children,
shewing to the generation to come the praises
of the LORD, and his **strength**, *and his*
wonderful works that he hath done.

We know that God works in our generations
and we pray regularly for them that they will
serve the Lord and make Heaven as we did.
God gives us strength to believe this. So let's
declare this today:

"I declare the Lord God will not hide
anything from our children or the
generations to come as we are
strengthened by His wondrous works
that He has done!"

IN JESUS NAME!

NO SIN
IS
ACCEPTABLE
TO GOD!

DAY THIRTY-NINE

Psalm 81:1
*Sing aloud unto God our **strength**: make a*
joyful noise unto the God of Jacob.

We know that our songs sung in praise to God
strengthen us as we make a joyful noise unto
Him. We don't have to be a perfect pitch
singer to give praise to the Lord but just a
person making a joyful noise headed towards
Heaven. So let's declare this today:

"I declare as we sing unto the Lord
making a joyful noise we shall be
strengthened!"

IN JESUS NAME!

JESUS IS
OUR HEALER,
OUR DELIVERER!

DAY FORTY

Psalm 84:5
*Blessed is the man whose **strength** is in thee;*
in whose heart are the ways of them.

God's blessings require us to be strong and endure the race. Our hearts must continuously be checked and cleansed before God on a daily basis because our God is a holy God. So let's declare this today:

"I declare the blessing over me as God has my heart and is strengthening it to receive!"

IN JESUS NAME!

THE LORD WILL RENEW
YOUR YOUTH
LIKE THE EAGLES!

DAY FORTY-ONE

Psalm 103:20
Bless the LORD, ye his angels, that excel
*in **strength**, that do his commandments,*
hearkening unto the voice of his word.

God gives us strength through His ministering
angels in times of need. Jesus was ministered
to by them in the desert after the devil
tempted Him. Today they minister to the
saints as well. So let's declare this today:

"I declare that the Lord be blessed
because His angels which excel in
strength minister unto me at the voice
of His Word!"

IN JESUS NAME!

THE LORD WILL
SATISFY
YOU WITH
LONG LIFE!

DAY FORTY-TWO

Psalm 105:4
*Seek the LORD, and his **strength**: seek his*
face evermore.

There are many ways God gives us strength
and in many instances He will do so. But how
best is it to receive this strength? Seek the
Lord, His strength and His face forevermore.
So let's declare this today:

**"I declare I will seek the face of the
Lord and His strength!"**

IN JESUS NAME!

JESUS IS
THE ROSE OF SHARON
AND
THE LILY OF THE VALLEY!

DAY FORTY-THREE

Psalm 118:14
*The LORD is my **strength** and song, and is*
become my salvation.

Every day we have a need for strength as we
sing a sweet song praising God for our
salvation and our need fades away and the
glory of the Lord comes. We are set free. So
let's declare this today:

"I declare we sing a song of salvation
and the Lord is our strength!"

IN JESUS NAME!

LAUGH YOUR WAY
TO
A STRONG HEART!

DAY FORTY-FOUR

Psalm 119:28
My soul melteth for heaviness: **strengthen**
thou me according unto thy word.

Our soul is in the Lord's hands when we give it
over to Him in salvation and surrender. The
Word of God will charter our path before us.
So let's declare this today:

**"I declare I have had heaviness in my
soul but Your Word shall strengthen
me!"**

IN JESUS NAME!

THERE IS
NO RIDICULE
IN THE
SON THAT RULES!

DAY FORTY-FIVE

Psalm 132:8
*Arise, O LORD, into thy rest; thou, and the ark
of thy **strength**.*

The ark is evident throughout scripture that
held Noah and His family and then another
ark was The Ark of the Covenant which
carried holy things of God. Nonetheless this
scripture states we have an ark of strength
which we carry because of the peace and rest
God gives us. We are His ark here on earth
now. We carry His presence. So let's declare
this today:

*"I declare Lord when you arise into
your rest, that you are the ark of my
strength!"*

IN JESUS NAME!

YOU HAVE
TREASURES
LAID UP
IN HEAVEN!

DAY FORTY-SIX

Psalm 144:1
Blessed be the LORD my **strength** *which*
teacheth my hands to war, and my fingers to
fight:

Thank God He gives us strength to battle by
praying and believing in Him as Victorious
Warrior because the battle belongs to the
Lord. So let's declare this today:

"I declare the Lord is blessed and His
strength teaches me how to war with
my hands and my fingers to fight as I
pray!"

IN JESUS NAME!

THE LORD
IS
HIGH
AND LIFTED UP!

DAY FORTY-SEVEN

Psalm 24:8
Who is this King of
glory? The LORD **strong** *and*
mighty, the LORD mighty in battle.

The Lord gives us strength for the daily battles
of life, but we could not do it without Him.
The Lord is mighty and we are not, for he is
the King of Glory. So let's declare this today:

**"I declare the King of Glory is the
LORD strong and mighty and He will
fight my battles and I am His!"**

IN JESUS NAME!

JESUS
WILL
SAVE
YOUR
CHILDREN!

DAY FORTY-EIGHT

Psalm 31:21
Blessed be the LORD: for he hath shewed me
*his marvellous kindness in a **strong** city.*

How many know the Lord can be strong for
you anywhere you are at? He is so kind to put
us in a strong city to keep us safe from any
enemy of our souls. He is our salvation. So
let's declare this today:

"I declare the blessing of the Lord
because He has shown me marvelous
things while keeping me safe in a
strong city!"

IN JESUS NAME!

THE LORD
HAS GIVEN
US
ETERNAL LIFE!

DAY FORTY-NINE

Proverbs 17:22
A merry heart doeth good like a medicine:
but a broken spirit drieth the bones.

We must know that we as God's children have a remedy for sadness or dryness of spirit; it is laughter and joy as this scripture states very clearly. So let's declare this today:

"I declare that my heart is merry and laughter is like a good medicine but when I am broken hearted it dries the bones!"

IN JESUS NAME!

REJOICE
THE LORD
WILL COME
SOON!

DAY FIFTY

Joshua 1:6
*Be **strong** and of a good courage: for unto*
this people shalt thou divide for an
inheritance the land, which I sware unto their
fathers to give them.

God gives us the strength and courage because
we are His people. We are strong enough then
to receive the inheritance that He has for us.
So let's declare this today:

"I declare that I am strong and of a
good courage as God's people we will
receive the inheritance that was
promised to our fathers!"

IN JESUS NAME!

JESUS
IS
THE
SOON COMING
KING!

DAY FIFTY-ONE

2 Corinthians 12:9
*And he said unto me, My grace is sufficient for thee: for my **strength** is made perfect in weakness. Most gladly therefore will I rather glory in my infirmities, that the power of Christ may rest upon me.*

The Lord has reached down toward us and given us grace to keep us strong each and every day. His strength and His power are available to us and His grace is plenty to keep us that way. So let's declare this today:

"I declare the Lord's grace is sufficient for you and me today as we glory in His power that rests upon us!"

IN JESUS NAME!

JESUS
IS THE
BRIDEGROOM,
WE ARE
THE BRIDE!

DAY FIFTY-TWO

2 Corinthians 12:10
*Therefore I take pleasure in infirmities, in reproaches, in necessities, in persecutions, in distresses for Christ's sake: for when I am weak, then am I **strong**.*

Many times in life we need God to give us strength but the Bible says when we are weak He is strong and as our Father He reaches down and blesses us. So let's declare this today:

"I declare taking pleasure in my distresses for Christ's sake is easy because when I am weak, the LORD is strong!"

IN JESUS NAME!

THERE IS
ONLY
ONE WAY
LET'S
GO UP!

DAY FIFTY-THREE

Psalm 103:2
Bless the LORD, O my soul, and forget not all his benefits:

The Lord has given us so many benefits in His endless mercies are forever. We should be so thankful each and every day. So let's declare this today:

"I declare bless the Lord O my soul and I will not forget all of His many benefits!"

IN JESUS NAME!

WE WILL
LIVE
FOREVER!

DAY FIFTY-FOUR

Psalm 103:3
Who forgiveth all thine iniquities; who
healeth all thy diseases;

God forgives us through Jesus Christ our Lord
and Savior and heals all our diseases; what
can be better than that? Let's give Him some
praise for this! So let's declare this today:

**"I declare the LORD forgives all of my
iniquities and heals all my diseases!"**

IN JESUS NAME!

**JESUS
HAS COME
TO
SAVE ME!**

DAY FIFTY-FIVE

Psalm 103:4
Who redeemeth thy life from destruction;
who crowneth thee with lovingkindness and
tender mercies;

The Lord keeps providing for us in oh so many ways as He was the one who redeemed our lives. So let's declare this today:

"I declare Jesus redeemed my life from destruction and crowned me with His lovingkindness and tender mercies!"

IN JESUS NAME!

LET US
GO
TO THE CROSS
AND REPENT!

DAY FIFTY-SIX

Psalm 103:5
Who satisfieth thy mouth with good things;
so that thy youth is renewed like the eagle's.

The Lord gives us far reaching benefits to help us each and every day in our lives. So let's declare this today:

"I declare the LORD satisfies my mouth with good things and my youth shall be renewed like that of the eagle!"

IN JESUS NAME!

WE HAVE
THE HOLY SPIRIT
AND FIRE!

DAY FIFTY-SEVEN

Psalm 103:8
The LORD is merciful and gracious, slow to
anger, and plenteous in mercy.

The Lord is so good to us that in Psalm 103
there are many things these scriptures speak
of as He is merciful to us daily. So let's declare
this today:

"I declare the Lord is merciful and
gracious towards us and slow to anger
and had plenty of mercy to go around
for all of us!"

IN JESUS NAME!

THE LORD
FULL OF FIRE
HAS CONSUMED
MY DEBT!

DAY FIFTY-EIGHT

Psalm 103:20
Bless the LORD, ye his angels, that excel in
strength, that do his commandments,
hearkening unto the voice of his word

God gives us angels charge over us to
strengthen us and minister to us as in this
Psalm. Let us take heed and know that God is
watching over you and me who love Him. So
let's declare this today:

"I declare blessings unto the Lord and
His angels that excel in strength, that
do His commandments and obey the
voice of His word!"

IN JESUS NAME!

JUST
CRY OUT
THE NAME
OF JESUS!

DAY FIFTY-NINE

Psalm 103:21
Bless ye the LORD, all ye his hosts; ye
ministers of his, that do his pleasure.

Our God sends His angels to bless and
minister to us regularly and do His pleasure
for us. So let's declare this today:

"I declare bless the LORD and all His
angels (hosts) who minister to us and
do His pleasure for us!"

IN JESUS NAME!

SORROW
IS NOT
MY PORTION!

DAY SIXTY

Psalm 103:22
Bless the LORD, all his works in all places of
his dominion: bless the LORD, O my soul.

When we keep blessing the Lord as in Psalm
103, He keeps blessing us and He will have
dominion over our soul, and how many know
this is a good thing? So let's declare this today:

"I declare bless the LORD, all works
that He has dominion over, blesses the
LORD O my soul!"

IN JESUS NAME!

NO MORE
EXCUSES
MARCH
FORWORD!

ACKNOWLEDGMENTS

We would like to acknowledge our publishers in: **Simply This Publishing** and **Pastor John Perry** for all of his publishing help.

We would like to acknowledge the **Second Saturday Sisters**; our church women's group for taste-testing this book on Saturday, September 11th, 2021 in our monthly meeting. Thanks for the thumbs-up!

We would like to acknowledge **Pastors William & Pauline White** who keep us on the road of straight and narrow truth and teach us good things in our church. We love you & Edgewater Church of God!

We would like to acknowledge **Dr. Frank & Karen Sumrall** who ordained us in 2015 and who had faith in God for us and has

maintained a beloved friendship towards us.
God bless you!

Proverbs 3:4-6
4 So shalt thou find favour and good
understanding in the sight of God and man.

5 Trust in the LORD *with all thine heart; and*
lean not unto thine own understanding.

6 In all thy ways acknowledge him, and he
shall direct thy paths.

AUTHOR'S CORNER

Susan Perry lives and writes in Edgewater, Florida with her husband John R. Perry. They publish books together in the gift God has given them in: **Simply This Publishing.**

Their lives are full as they continue to praise and worship God in all that they do; the Bible says that God inhabits our praises.

Psalm 22:3
But thou art holy, O thou that inhabitest the praises of Israel.

John & Susan have four children in their blended marriage and so far 5 grandchildren and blessed by each and every one. They all live scattered throughout the United States and they visit when they can. Vacations are often a family affair. They attend Edgewater

Church of God, and their Pastor is Bishop William T. White.

The Lord has spoken to them to write and publish others and they continue on this path today. They both have seen God heal people as they lay hands upon them. They have always desired a healing ministry from the Lord and so far these past few years they have grown in this.

James 5:14-16
14 Is any sick among you? let him call for the elders of the church; and let them pray over him, anointing him with oil in the name of the Lord:

15 And the prayer of faith shall save the sick, and the Lord shall raise him up; and if he have committed sins, they shall be forgiven him.

16 Confess your faults one to another, and pray one for another, that ye may be healed. The effectual fervent prayer of a righteous man availeth much.

Their faith has increased as well as their ministry to love and obey God staying humbly before the Throne. Their goal is to please Jesus as others needs are met through their ministry of love and hope. At one time the

Lord spoke to Susan and said: *"Be Ministers of Hope."*

Hebrews 6:19-20
19 This hope we have as an anchor of the soul, both sure and steadfast, and which enters the Presence behind the veil,

20 where the forerunner has entered for us, even Jesus, having become High Priest forever according to the order of Melchizedek.

IN JESUS NAME, AMEN!

PERRY'S BOOK SHELF

The Samaritan Woman Testifies
Kindle only: $9.95

Simply This: The World's Greatest Message
Paperback: $5.95 Kindle: $3.99

Preach It Sister Girl!
Paperback: $9.95 Kindle: $5.99

ASK for WISDOM: The Safe Harbor of God
Paperback: $9.95 Kindle: $5.99

A Stone's Throw Away: A Woman Testifies
Paperback: $12.95 Kindle: $6.99

The Persistent Widow Testifies
Paperback: $12.95 Kindle: $6.99

**The Woman Presenting the Alabaster Box
Testifies**
Paperback: $12.95 Kindle: $6.99

Great Holes in Your Pockets: Recovering All!
Paperback: $9.95 Kindle $5.99

Hidden in the Cleft of the Rock: A Woman Testifies
Paperback: $12.95 Kindle: $6.99

Daughters of Inheritance Testify
Paperback: $12.95 Kindle: $6.99

This Project is Called: HONOR
Paperback: $9.95 Kindle: $5.99

Our Experiences With ANGELS
Paperback $9.95 Kindle $5.99

The Double-Dip Blessings
Paperback $9.95 Kindle $5.99

It's Never Too Late To Pray
Paperback $5.95 Kindle $2.99

I AM A DUCK!
Paperback $9.95 Kindle $5.95

The Woman Touching the Hem of His Garment Testifies
Paperback $12.95 Kindle $6.99

"This is the Anemic Church!"
Paperback $9.95 Kindle $5.99

There is a Witness!
Paperback $9.95 Kindle $5.99

Heal Them All! The Children's Portion
Paperback $7.95 Kindle $3.99

Ye Shall Serve GOD On This Mountain
Paperback $12.95 Kindle $6.99

Thanksgiving is Best!
Paperback $7.95 Kindle $3.99

The ABC'S of Perry
Paperback $12.95

LOVE is Surely the Way!
Paperback $7.95 Kindle $3.99

Lessons In Deliverance
Paperback $12.95 Kindle $6.99

Cancel Cancer: And The Effects Thereof
Paperback $9.95 Kindle $5.99

Royalty BELONGS To The Believer!
Paperback $9.95 Kindle $5.99

"Just When Did This Happen??" Examining Senior Moments
Paperback $9.95 Kindle $5.99

I Declare Over You: In Jesus Name
Paperback $5.95 Kindle $2.99

Going Down The Barker Road, Missing...
Paperback $9.95 Kindle $5.99

Deception of Man: Sin Lies At The Door
Paperback $12.95 Kindle $6.99 Hardcover $15.95

Beautiful Things: Out Of The Dust
Paperback $9.95 Kindle $5.99

Trauma: The Doors Opened To A Unique Spirit

Paperback $12.95 Kindle $6.99

In My Weakness God is Strong: Declarations of Strength

Paperback $15.95 Kindle $8.99

CONTACT THE PERRYS:

1 Corinthians 14:3
But he who prophesies speaks edification and
exhortation and comfort to men

All books available on www.Amazon.com
Kindle Direct Publishing

Simply This Publishing

John & Susan Perry
Edgewater, Florida

Contact info:

Susan J Perry, Email:
susiebqt987p@yahoo.com
& Facebook

John R Perry, Email: jperry8@bellsouth.net

Amazon Author Page link:

https://www.amazon.com/Susan-J-
Perry/e/B08V5B67QT?ref_=dbs_p_pbk_r00
_abau_000000

Books can also be ordered through bookstores
and big box stores if that is your preference.
There is always a way.

In Florida our books are available in:

From My Library 2 URS

3510 S Nova Road, Suite # 107

Port Orange, Florida 32129

RESOURCES

Wikipedia online research

Bible Gateway online Bible scripture research

The King James Study Bible for Women

Webster and Oxford Dictionary online definitions

Crosswalk.com

Black & White online free clipart

Amazon online website

Jeremiah 29:11
"For I know the plans I have for you,"
declares the L*ORD*, *"plans to*
prosper you and not to harm you,
plans to give you hope and a future."

GOD WILL
LIFT US UP
OUT OF
THE MIRY CLAY,
SELAH!

Made in the USA
Coppell, TX
28 June 2022

79303320R20079